The Great British Quiz Book

This Armada book belongs to:

_____

_____

_____

Jonathan Clements is the author of a number of books, including two other original Armadas – *The Armada Book of Jokes and Riddles* and *Crazy – But True!* (a collection of curious and fantastic facts). He was born in Cornwall and he and his wife now live in Wiltshire. He says that his favourite place in Britain is Stonehenge, his favourite meal is fish and chips, and his favourite sport is playing in his annual village football match.

on the cover: John Bull, the Royal Standard, Edward VII, Winston Churchill, Coronation Issue of the Daily Express, Charles Dickens, St Paul's Cathedral

THE
GREAT
BRITISH
QUIZ
BOOK

Jonathan Clements

An Original Armada

The Great British Quiz Book was
first published 1975 in Armada by
William Collins Sons & Co. Ltd.,
14 St. James's Place, London, SW1A 1PF

© Jonathan Clements 1975
An Original Armada

Printed in Great Britain by
Love & Malcomson Ltd., Brighton Road,
Redhill, Surrey.

Name the Counties

Here are the outlines of 8 counties—Wiltshire, Suffolk, Devon, Northampton, Herefordshire, Perthshire, Sussex and Yorkshire. Can you match each county with its place on the map?

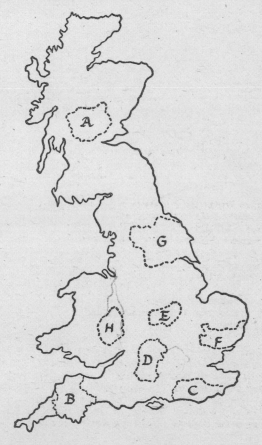

2 Bridges and Tunnels

1. Which famous English bridge was sold to America in 1971?

2. Where is the Royal Albert bridge?

3. When was the first iron bridge built: (a) 1654? (b) 1779? or (c) 1821?

4. Which is the longest railway tunnel in the British Isles?

5. Who designed the Clifton Suspension bridge?

6. Which bridge in London opens upwards to allow tall ships to pass by?

7. Where is the Blackwall tunnel?

8. Which is the odd bridge out: Tamar? Wadebridge? Iron-bridge?

9. How long is the Severn tunnel: (a) 4 miles? (b) 6 miles? or (c) 8 miles?

10. What were most Roman bridges built of?

11. Which famous Scottish bridge collapsed in 1863?

12. Which famous football team play near Putney bridge?

Can you give the name for a person who lives in each of these places?

1. Oxford

2. Liverpool

3. Halifax

4. Manchester

5. London

6. Devon

7. Wales

8. Aberdeen

9. Cambridge

10. Isle of Man

11. Dublin

12. Glasgow

4 Down By the Riverside

1. Which is the longest river in the British Isles?

2. Which river flows through London?

3. On which river does Chester stand?

4. Which two cities are linked by the Grand Union Canal?

5. How long is the river Severn: (a) 220 miles? (b) 400 miles? or (c) 672 miles?

6. In which county does the river Trent rise?

7. Is the Serpentine situated on the river Thames?

8. Which one of these rivers flows directly into the sea: (a) Eden? (b) Aire? or (c) Weaver?

9. Which river flows through Canterbury?

10. On which river does Derby stand?

11. Name the rivers of which these are tributaries: (a) Cherwell (b) Trent.

12. How many locks are there on the Worcester and Birmingham Canal: (a) 17? (b) 30? or (c) 42?

Find the Statesman

Take the letters in the name of each object from the word on the left, and write the remaining letter in the end column. You'll then find a famous British statesman.

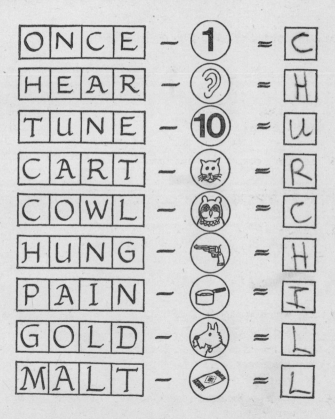

ONCE − (1) = C

HEAR − (ear) = H

TUNE − (10) = U

CART − (cat) = R

COWL − (owl) = C

HUNG − (gun) = H

PAIN − (pan) = I

GOLD − (dog) = L

MALT − (mat) = L

6 Museums and Art Galleries

1. In which museum can the Elgin Marbles be seen?

2. How many museums and galleries are there in the British Isles: (a) 2000? (b) 1000? or (c) 500?

3. In which city is the National Portrait Gallery?

4. Where can you see John Constable's famous painting 'The Hay Wain'?

5. In which museum will you find the 105ft long skeleton of a dinosaur?

6. Which famous art gallery is situated on the Millbank, London?

7. Where would you find a museum devoted to Samuel Johnson?

8. What unusual kind of collection is housed at the Valhalla Museum, Tresco, Scilly Isles?

9. Was the British Museum opened in (a) 1759? (b) 1859? (c) 1901?

10. Which London museum is devoted solely to railways?

11. Where is the Manx Museum?

12. Which is the biggest waxworks collection in Great Britain?

Mr and Miss-Quote

See if you can spot the deliberate mistake in each of these famous British quotations. Just one word in each is wrong. Can you replace it with the correct one?

1. "I wandered lonely as a lollipop."

2. "A thing of beauty is a deckchair forever."

3. "Shall I compare thee to a summer's frog?"

4. "How do I love thee? Let me count the radishes."

5. "She walks in beauty like the omnibus."

6. "Stands the grandfather clock at ten to three."

7. "And did those knees in ancient time."

8. "The drunkard tolls the knell of parting day."

9. "If you can keep your trousers when all about you are losing theirs."

10. "My love is like a red, red pomegranate."

11. "Come into the refrigerator, Maud."

12. "Drink to me only with thine ears."

8 Abbreviated English

Do you know what these widely-used initials stand for?

1. M.C.C.

2. Q.C.

3. B.A.

4. H.R.H.

5. A.W.O.L.

6. F.A.

7. R.S.P.C.A.

8. M.P.

9. R.A.

10. O.H.M.S.

11. M.B.E.

12. L.T.A.

These four signposts have very strange names on them. If you re-arrange the letters on each sign correctly, you'll find out to which towns in England they point.

> ## Flogdubir   16

> ## Hideleffs   5

> ## Slowgag   7

> ## Whipsci   2

See if you can find the missing word (a place in the British Isles) in each of the following song titles:

1. "It's a Long Way to ————."

2. "I Belong to ————."

3. "Maybe It's Because I'm A ————."

4. "Kelly From the Isle of ————."

5. "———— Central."

6. "The ———— Races."

7. "———— by the Sea."

8. "———— Cathedral."

9. "The ——— Boating Song."

10. "The Wombles of ———— Common."

11. "The Leaving of ————."

12. The Rose of ————."

Island Lore 11

1. How many islands does the British Isles consist of: (a) 1500? (b) 5000? or (c) 7000?

2. On which island is the resort of Shanklin?

3. Which is the odd island out: (a) Hayling, (b) Beetroot, (c) Canvey, (d) Arran?

4. Name two of the largest Channel islands

5. What is the island near Penzance in Cornwall called?

6. What is the Isle of Dogs?

7. Where is Fair Isle?

8. Which animal is the Isle of Man famous for?

9. How many islands in Great Britain are inhabited: (a) 200? (b) 300? or (c) 400?

10. Are the Shetland Isles part of the British Isles?

11. Where is the Isle of Sheppey?

12. In which ocean is the island of Rockall?

12 Highways and Byways

1. Where is the longest hill in the British Isles?

2. What did J. L. Macadam invent?

3. Between which cities does the M1 motorway run?

4. What is the approximate distance by road between London and Penzance?

5. When were milestones first used: (a) 1610? (b) 1727? or (c) 1814?

6. What is a 'drove' road?

7. Can one drive a car along a bridle-path?

8. What were 'turnpike' roads?

9. What is the approximate distance between Cardiff and Edinburgh?

10. When were the first traffic lights installed in Britain: (a) 1868? (b) 1905? or (c) 1920?

11. Is it true that there was no road speed limit in 1897?

12. How can you get out of a *cul-de-sac* road?

Can you find the old English proverb hidden in this circle?
Take all the letters of each different type of lettering, and
make one word out of them. By arranging the words correctly, you'll be able to make the proverb.

14   Old Britain

1. Was Lady Godiva real or fictitious?

2. Was a 'churl': (a) a scaffold; (b) a frog or (c) a peasant?

3. What long poem is Geoffery Chaucer famous for?

4. Which king signed the Magna Carta?

5. What plague killed two million people in England in the 15th century?

6. Who was King of England at the time of the Norman Conquest?

7. When was the longbow invented: (a) 1153? (b) 1346? or (c) 1420?

8. Which king is reputed to have burnt some cakes?

9. Who was Wat Tyler?

10. Which city was the capital of Wessex?

11. Who wrote 'Piers Plowman'?

12. Which king is supposed to have ordered the sea to retreat?

London Life 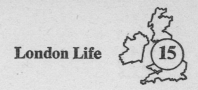 15

1. With what do you associate Harley Street?

2. Where would you find the grave of Karl Marx?

3. Where is the second biggest collection of books in the world kept?

4. What is the official name for Westminster Abbey?

5. Where is London's biggest rugby football ground?

6. What is Savile Row famous for?

7. Where is Cleopatra's Needle?

8. Were the Houses of Parliament built in: (a) 1770? (b) 1810? or (c) 1840?

9. What famous cricket ground is at St John's Wood?

10. In which London area are most of the big museums to be found?

11. What were the first London policemen called?

12. In which London street did Conan Doyle's famous detective Sherlock Holmes live?

16 Match the Names

Below are given twelve surnames of famous Britons of the past. Match them up with their correct Christian names.

1. CROMWELL   (a) *Horatio*

2. WORDSWORTH   (b) *Samuel*

3. CHURCHILL   (c) *Edward*

4. BRUNEL   (d) *Oliver*

5. DISRAELI   (e) *George*

6. KITCHENER   (f) *Rudyard*

7. MILTON   (g) *Winston*

8. BADEN-POWELL   (h) *William*

9. STUBBS   (i) *Isambard*

10. LEAR   (j) *Benjamin*

11. PEPYS   (k) *Robert*

12. KIPLING   (l) *John*

Fact or Fallacy? 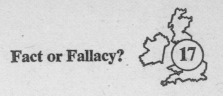 17

Simply answer True or False to the following statements:

1. Sandwiches were invented by the Earl of Sandwich

2. In 1971, a statue of Lord Nelson in Dublin was blown up

3. Nylon stockings are made partly out of coal

4. China clay comes mostly from Cornwall

5. Woollen socks are made out of coconuts

6. Quicksands suck a victim downwards

7. Paper can be made out of wood

8. Birmingham is at the exact centre of England

9. The bagpipe is a Scottish invention

10. Henry VII had only one ear

11. Photography was invented in Wiltshire in 1835

12. The first ever radio transmission was sent across England

18 Bird Changes

Add the letters in the given word to the bird's name to get the word indicated by the clue on the right.

Add LAWS to and get another bird

Add WIN to and get a fool

Add HOOD to and get an outlaw

Add AGE to 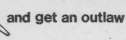 and get a south-coast town

Can you fill in the missing partners?

1. Gilbert and ————

2. Tweedledum and ————

3. Tristan and ————

4. Pomp and ————

5. Dr Jekyll and ————

6. Scotch and ————

7. Holmes and ————

8. Punch and ————

9. Lancelot and ————

10. Jack and ————

11. Flanagan and ————

12. Darby and ————

20 Great British Grub

See if you can complete these phrases. All of them are names of very popular British dishes.

1. Bangers and ————

2. Roast beef and ————

3. Fish and ————

4. Prunes and ————

5. Boiled beef and ————

6. Strawberries and ————

7. Tripe and ————

8. Cheese and ————

9. Bacon and ————

10. Bubble and ————

11. Toast and ————

12. Stew and ————

Can you match the names to these four counties (which are all bounded by water on at least one side).

Dorset, Cornwall, Norfolk, Hampshire.

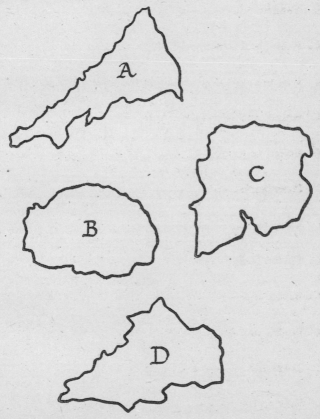

22 Castles and Monuments

1. What is Blarney Castle famous for?

2. Where did many of the stones for Stonehenge come from?

3. What are the three main 'Ages' ancient history refers to?

4. Where would a portcullis be found in a castle?

5. What is Silbury Hill, in Wiltshire?

6. Which is the largest castle in England?

7. At which castle was Mary Tudor proclaimed Queen?

8. Where in Cornwall is King Arthur's castle supposed to have been?

9. What would you find at Chysauster, Cornwall?

10. Which is the odd castle out: Conway, Windsor, Caernarvon, Harlech.

11. Which is the largest castle in Scotland?

12. What is the 'keep' of a castle?

Black Britain

Each of the following names or descriptions should suggest a phrase containing the word 'black'. See how many you can get right.

1. The Bubonic Plague

2. Most famous horse in English literature

3. Disgrace to the family

4. The Irish Constabulary

5. Scottish Highlanders

6. Prison van

7. Popular dance of the 1920s.

8. Illegal trade

9. Famous English pirate

10. Bird with an orange beak

11. Disapproving stare

12. Air-raid precaution

Name the Creature

Here are some definitions of well-known phrases. Each phrase contains the name of a British animal (bird, beast or fish). See how many you can find.

1. A gathering of women

2. A sociable old man

3. A driver with bad manners

4. One who gets up at dawn

5. A thief who climbs in through windows

6. A very small person

7. A motionless target

8. A disgrace to the family

9. A tireless labourer

10. One who stays up late

11. A bad-tempered person

12. A chronic over-eater

Here's a collection of popular British slang words. See if you can pick out the correct meaning of each word.

1. CONK   (a)nose (b)head (c)dustbin

2. BOBBY   (a)policeman (b)earwig (c)taxi-driver

3. QUID   (a)fish (b)pound note (c)kettle

4. SCARPER   (a)run away (b)walk (c)eskimo

5. FOURPENNY-ONE   (a)stutter (b)kick (c)punch

6. KIP   (a)sleep (b)jump (c)read

7. NARKED   (a)pleased (b)annoyed (c)knocked out

8. ACKERS   (a)gnome (b)trousers (c)money

9. WALLOP   (a)tree (b)beer (c)wine

10. SCUPPERED   (a)fooled (b)beaten (c)deafened

11. FOUR EYES   (a)owl (b)bespectacled person (c)photographer

12. TIPSY   (a)drunk (b)dancing (c)hungry

Can you find the old English proverb hidden here? There are five interlocking shapes—each shape contains the letters which will make up one word of the proverb.

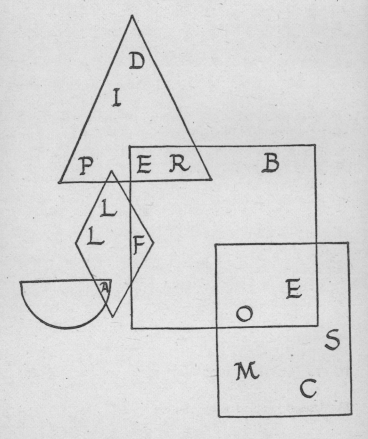

White Britain

Each of the following names or descriptions should suggest a phrase containing the word 'white'. See how many you can get right.

1. A government report

2. A novel by Wilkie Collins

3. British government offices

4. 'Alice Through the Looking-Glass' character

5. A very small fib

6. Expression of cowardice

7. An East London district

8. Spurs football club

9. Scottish evergreen tree

10. A Briton's penance

11. To make respectable

12. Useless jumble-sale bargain

Mountains Tall

1. Which is the highest mountain in England?

2. Where are the Cleveland Hills?

3. In which county is Ben Lomond?

4. Which two mountains in Great Britain have railways to their summits?

5. Which is the highest mountain in Wales?

6. What are the 'Seven Sisters'?

7. In which county are the Cheviot mountains?

8. How many mountains over 4,000 feet high are there in Scotland: (a) 2? (b) 4? or (c) 10?

9. Which is the highest mountain in Ireland?

10. Which is the odd mountain out: Skiddaw, Ben Nevis, Helvellyn, Great Gable.

11. Which is the highest mountain in Scotland?

12. Where is Box Hill?

How Well Do You Know England?

 (29)

1. In which county is Gatwick Airport?

2. Which is further east—Newcastle or Portsmouth?

3. Complete the names of these 'county' foods: ————— pasty, ————— pudding

4. Can you name any of the Scilly Isles?

5. Which is the odd one out: Reading, Canterbury, Taunton, Trowbridge

6. Which is the most densely populated county?

7. Where is the Solent?

8. Which is further west—Bristol or Liverpool?

9. How long is the English coastline: (a) 3500 miles? (b) 2800 miles? or (c) 1800 miles?

10. What have these in common: Pentop Pike, Rowridge, Holme Moss

11. Where are the Fens?

12. Which is the largest county in England?

B

If you start on the correct letter, and always move to an adjacent square (horizontally, vertically or diagonally), you can discover the names of five British birds. Use all the letters, but no letter more than once.

I	B	G	L	W
N	O	A	E	O
H	R	E	T	L
E	N	T	I	L
R	O	S	W	A

Railway Excursions

1. Where is the famous 'Bluebell' line?

2. When did the first passenger train run: (a) 1825? (b) 1871? or (c) 1888?

3. Which is the busiest railway junction in England?

4. Who invented the steam-driven railway engine?

5. Which new underground system is being built now in London?

6. Which is the longest railway bridge in the British Isles?

7. Which is the newest London railway station?

8. Name two regions British Railways

9. Who built the railway bridge over the river Tamar?

10. Between which two places is the longest possible railway journey in Great Britain?

11. Which is the highest point at sea-level reached on British Railways: (a) 710ft? (b) 1105ft? or (c) 1484ft?

12. Which London main line station has the name of a saint?

32 How Well Do You Know Scotland?

1. What is John O' Groats famous for?

2. Which is further south—Edinburgh or Glasgow?

3. What is a sporran?

4. Who was John Knox?

5. Which is the biggest Scottish county?

6. Is a caber (a) a bird? (b) a long pole? or (c) a dress?

7. What is the name of Scotland's largest football stadium?

8. What famous building is at Balmoral?

9. In which county is Dundee?

10. Are the Orkneys and Shetlands part of Scotland?

11. Who was Flora Macdonald?

12. What is the musical instrument unique to Scotland?

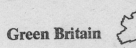
Each of the following names or descriptions should suggest a phrase containing the word 'green'. See how many you can get right.

1. Robin Hood's colour

2. A runaway marriage to Scotland

3. A small kind of plum

4. Author of 'Our Man In Havana'

5. A park near Buckingham Palace

6. Vegetable seller

7. Jealousy

8. Irish song

9. What every good gardener has

10. Proverb about comparisons

11. 16th Century heroine in song

12. Boy Scout song about rushes

Can you make 30 or more words out of

PRESTON

(Each word must contain at least four letters, and no letter may be used more than once in the same word)

REST	ETON	
NOTE	NEST	
TOONE	STEN	
POET	STONE	
PEST	SPOT	
STEP	PERSON	
POST	POTS	
STOP	RENT	
NOSE	RENTS	
NORSE		

Each of the following names or descriptions should suggest a phrase containing the word 'blue'. See how many you can get right.

1. The symbol of a British police station

2. An intellectual woman

3. Architect's plans

4. Scottish song

5. A nursery rhyme lad

6. Expression meaning 'seldom'

7. Person of high social standing

8. To edit

9. To be extravagant

10. A prize

11. Coventry football club

12. Sailors

36 Parliament Posers

1. Where are the Houses of Parliament situated?

2. Name the three main political parties

3. Who was the leader of the Conservative party in 1966?

4. Was Samuel Pepys ever a M.P.?

5. Which of these constituencies doesn't exist: Orkney and Shetland, All Saints, Balls Pond Road

6. Which of these are *not* allowed to vote at General Elections: Peers, lunatics, clergymen, aliens

7. What is the Prime Minister's official address?

8. What is the name of the Prime Minister's country house?

9. How many Prime Ministers have there been since 1730: (a) 30? (b) 50? or (c) 62?

10. Who were the Conservative, Labour and Liberal leaders in 1973?

11. What is the maximum period of a Parliament under one party?

12. Who held the office of Prime Minister the greatest number of times?

Fictional Folk

Can you name the authors who created these memorable characters in their books?

1. William Brown

2. Macbeth

3. The Hobbit

4. Dr Watson

5. James Bond

6. David Copperfield

7. The Mad Hatter

8. Bathsheba Everdene

9. Mole

10. Dr Finlay

11. Sadie Thompson

12. Jeeves

British Inventions

Were these machines, objects, sports, etc., invented in Great Britain? Just answer Yes or No to each invention.

1. Television

2. Photography

3. Cinematography

4. Tennis

5. Gramophones

6. Steam Locomotives

7. Radio

8. Football

9. Aeroplanes

10. Golf

11. Gunpowder

12. Fountain Pens

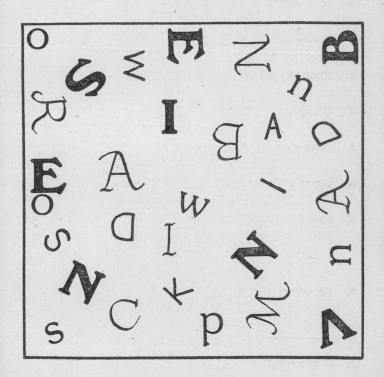

If you collect each group of letters together (there are four groups) and arrange them correctly, you'll find the names of four British mountains or mountain ranges.

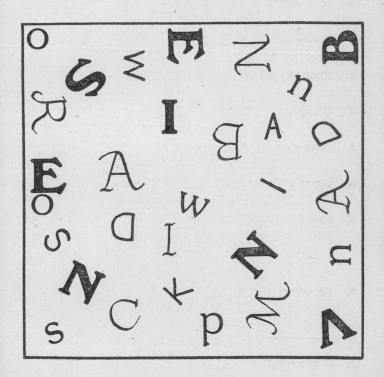

40 Pick the Plants

1. Which tree is the odd one out: cedar, birch, pine, cypress?

2. What is fungus?

3. Where is the New Forest?

4. Is the 'Angel's Fishing Rod' a real flower?

5. Name two of the most popular members of the rose family of trees

6. What wood is used for making cricket bats?

7. Which wild flower has a special day all of its own?

8. What is honeysuckle also known as?

9. Which flower is the odd one out: bluebell, sweet pea, laburnum, broom?

10. In which county is the Forest of Dean?

11. What wood was used in the making of longbows?

12. Give the proper name for the 'monkey puzzle' tree

Each of the following names or descriptions should suggest a phrase containing the word 'red'. See how many you can get right.

1. A nursery tale girl

2. Health organisation

3. A circus clown often has one

4. A false clue

5. A 17th century British soldier

6. A story featuring Sherlock Holmes

7. Robin

8. A terrific day

9. To extend a lavish welcome

10. The traffic signal which means 'Stop'

11. Bureaucratic delays

12. Caught in the act

42 Seaside Rock

By re-arranging the letters on the labels, see if you can work out where these jars of seaside rock came from.

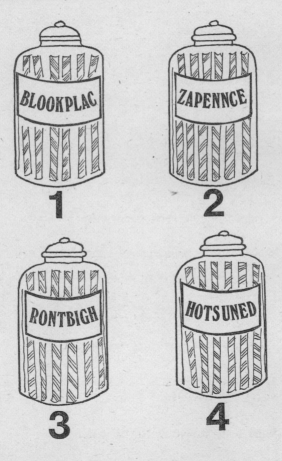

How Well Do You Know Ireland?

1. What is Ireland's main airport?

2. Is a shillelagh (a) a building? (b) an animal? or (c) a wooden club?

3. Name one of the four provinces of Ireland

4. In which county is Killarney?

5. What colour do Ireland's football team play in?

6. What is the national emblem of Ireland?

7. Is Londerry in Northern or Southern Ireland?

8. When was the great famine in Ireland: (a) 1722? (b) 1845? or (c) 1916?

9. In which county is Enniskillen?

10. What is Ireland's main passenger sea-port?

11. Is a jaunting-car: (a) a boat? (b) a horse-drawn cart? or (c) a vintage bike?

12. What is the capital of Northern Ireland?

44 Churches and Cathedrals

1. Which cathedral in Great Britain has the tallest spire?

2. What are church bells made of?

3. Who designed St Paul's Cathedral?

4. Which is the newest cathedral in Britain?

5. What is a lych-gate?

6. How many cathedrals are there in the British Isles: (a) 77? (b) 86? or (c) 110?

7. What is the popular definition of a Cockney?

8. How many lessons are read during a normal Church of England service?

9. Which are the two English cathedrals with three spires each?

10. In which Abbey would you find 'Poet's Corner'?

11. Which is the largest bell in Great Britain?

12. Which cathedral in England had its spire added 100 years after it was built?

Can you turn the squiggly lines below into the names of four large British cities, simply by adding 13 straight lines?

3ristoı

lulı

Jorʌ

3aın

46 Football Colours

Name the colours of the shirts of these famous football clubs.

1. Newcastle

2. Aston Villa

3. Sunderland

4. Arsenal

5. Chelsea

6. Celtic

7. Liverpool

8. Blackburn Rovers

9. Manchester City

10. Norwich

11. Leeds

12. West Bromwich Albion

Geological Games 47

Answer True or False to the following:

1. Cornwall is the most important county for tin mining

2. Fossilized dinosaurs have been found in England

3. Grains of sand are bigger than grains of gravel

4. South Wales is Britain's chief coal-mining area

5. Gold deposits have been found in Cambridge

6. The Cambrian period came before the Carboniferous period

7. A 'drumlin' is a small hill formed by the movement of ice

8. China clay is found in Berkshire

9. Westminster Abbey is built of limestone

10. The Houses of Parliament are built of granite

11. The Ice Age lasted from 1710 to 1780

12. Coal is formed mainly from the debris of old forests

48 Scenery and Greenery

1. Where is the 'Devil's Punchbowl'?

2. What have the following in common: St David's Head, Worm's Head, Great Ormes Head?

3. What is the name of the huge basalt pillars on the Antrim coast?

4. Where is the 'Hog's Back'?

5. An inlet on the coast, caused by the submerging of a valley, is called—what?

6. In which county is the 'Devil's Dyke'?

7. What are the main features of a glaciated valley?

8. Where can deer be found in Surrey?

9. In which county would you find Mullion Cove?

10. Which is the odd one out: Seat Sandal, Dollywagon Pike, Dunmail Raise?

11. Is 'scree' (a) an avalanche? (b) small stones? or (c) a moorland stretch?

12. Where is the 'Old Man Of Hoy'?

Town Trades

Match each place with the object that is associated with it:

1.	Nottingham	a)	*Motor Cars*
2.	Shetland	b)	*Cheese*
3.	Grimsby	c)	*Steel*
4.	Glasgow	d)	*Newspapers*
5.	Cheddar	e)	*Glass*
6.	London	f)	*Lace*
7.	Waterford	g)	*Fish*
8.	Dagenham	h)	*Tweed*
9.	Stoke	i)	*Ponies*
10.	Hebrides	j)	*China*
11.	St Austell	k)	*Whisky*
12.	Birmingham	l)	*Clay*

Here is a list of famous British quotations and sayings. Pick their authors from the list below.

1. 'A thing of beauty is a joy forever.'

2. 'We shall fight on the beaches, we shall fight on the landing grounds."

3. 'A little learning is a dangerous thing.'

4. 'England expects every man will do his duty.'

5. 'You never had it so good.'

6. 'In the spring a young man's fancy lightly turns to thoughts of love.'

7. 'The road to hell is paved with good intentions.'

8. 'If you can keep your head, when all about you are losing theirs.'

9. 'Never put off until tomorrow what you can do today.'

10. 'And is there honey still for tea?'

Rudyard Kipling, Lord Nelson, Samuel Johnson, Lord Tennyson, Rupert Brooke, Alexander Pope, John Keats, Winston Churchill, Harold Macmillan, Lord Chesterfield.

These town houses are made out of the letters of the towns where they are situated. Can you find out the names of the towns by arranging the letters correctly?

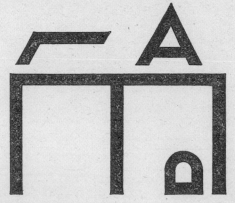

52 Weather Wise

Answer True or False to these statements:

1. Snow is frozen rain

2. It's warmer in the summer because Britain is nearer the sun then

3. Thunderstorms cause milk to go sour

4. It's dangerous to seek shelter under a tree in a storm

5. A ring around the moon is a sign of coming rain

6. Rainbows can be seen at night

7. Moonlit nights have the heaviest frosts

8. It is sometimes too cold to snow

9. Open windows attract lightning

10. Hail rarely falls during the winter

11. A change in the phase of the moon brings a change in the weather

12. Ireland has the highest rainfall in the British Isles

Industries and Agriculture 53

1. Where is the largest ship-building yard in Great Britain?

2. What is the main industry of Sheffield?

3. Which county in England has the most sheep?

4. Is the centre of the wool industry (a) Yorkshire? (b) Leeds? or (c) St Ives?

5. What kind of weather is needed to grow wheat?

6. Where is mustard mainly grown?

7. Which is the odd plant out: Jute, maize, flax?

8. What colour are Friesian cows?

9. What are the three main crops grown in Great Britain?

10. Where is the largest steel-works in Great Britain?

11. Which metal is Cornwall famous for mining?

12. Which industry employs the most workers: motors, chemicals, or printing?

Puzzling Professions

Three definitions are given for each of these British trades-men, etc. See if you can select the correct one.

1. OSTEOPATH — (a) painter (b) bone specialist (c) sink-unbunger

2. DERMATOLOGIST — (a) singer (b) butcher (c) skin specialist

3. WAINWRIGHT — (a) waiter (b) coffee-grinder (c) cart-maker

4. OSTLER — (a) stableman (b) auctioneer (c) card-player

5. TURNER — (a) contortionist (b) lathe worker (c) chef

6. TONSORIALIST — (a) opera singer (b) piano tuner (c) barber

7. BONIFACE — (a) innkeeper (b) plastic surgeon (c) sculptor

8. CHIROPODIST — (a) ear specialist (b) foot specialist (c) glass-blower

9. CHANDLER — (a) magician (b) chandelier-hanger (c) shopkeeper

10. LEXICOGRAPHER — (a) ambassador (b) dictionary-compiler (c) flea-trainer

11. PRESTIDGITATOR — (a) cartoonist (b) juggler (c) comedian

12. FARRIER — (a) blacksmith (b) pig breeder (c) salesman

Ports and Harbours 55

1. From which port would you sail to the Hook of Holland?

2. What have these four places in common: Chester, Seaford, Boston, Rye?

3. Name the port at the mouth of the river Tamar

4. Is a jetty (a) a lighthouse lamp? (b) a ship? or (c) a landing pier?

5. What is unusual about the streets in Clovelly, Devon?

6. Which is the largest port in the British Isles?

7. Name one of the 'Cinque' ports

8. From which port would you sail to Norway?

9. Which is the odd one out: Grimsby, Whitby, Aberdeen, Southampton?

10. From which ports in Great Britain can you sail to Ireland?

11. Was the first harbour in Great Britain built in: (a) 1610? (b) 1748? or (c) 1810?

12. Name the port at the mouth of the river Usk

56 Find the Places

In the empty space under each picture, write the first letter of the name of the object. If you do this correctly, you will have written the names of three towns and cities, reading across.

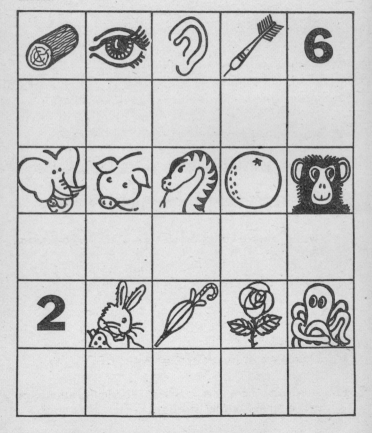

Here's a mixture of questions about Great Britain:

1. Was golf first played in Scotland?

2. Which English county is famous for cider?

3. What is the national flower of Scotland?

4. Are there any notable waterfalls in Derbyshire?

5. Which is the largest airport in the British Isles?

6. What is the approximate population of London?

7. Where are the Wightman Cup tennis matches held?

8. Which famous Irish author wrote the book 'Borstal Boy'?

9. Who was the last King of England?

10. Is Fuller's Earth a mineral product?

11. Do quinces grow in Great Britain?

12. How many lines does a colour television picture transmitted from London have?

1. In which year was decimal coinage introduced in Great Britain?

2. Before decimal coinage, how many pennies were there in a pound?

3. How much was a 'florin' worth?

4. How much was a 'shilling' worth?

5. What is a 1960's 'guinea' worth now?

6. What colour is a £5 note?

7. What is the thread running through a bank note made of?

8. How many sides did an old bronze threepenny bit have?

9. What colour is a £10 note?

10. Whose signature appears on bank notes?

11. In old money, how much was a 'dollar'?

12. How much is a 'pony'?

If you collect each group of letters together (there are four groups) and arrange them correctly, you'll find the names of four British fish.

60 City Sights

In which cities or towns in the British Isles would you find these well-known sights and landmarks?

1. The Royal Pavilion

2. The statue of Eros

3. Prince's Street

4. Trent Bridge cricket ground

5. The Gorbals

6. The 'Discovery'

7. The 'First and Last House in England'

8. Ninian Park football ground

9. The statue of George Washington

10. Drake's Drum

11. The Crown Jewels

12. The National Railway Museum

1. Who was the first Englishman to sail around the world?

2. What name is given to the stretch of water dividing England from France?

3. Who spent six months exploring New Zealand in 1769?

4. Which waterfall did Dr Livingstone discover in Africa?

5. Did the first English steamship cross the Atlantic in (a) 1821? (b) 1886? or (c) 1906?

6. What are the two most recent discoveries in the North Sea?

7. In what measurement are ocean depths taken?

8. What kind of ship is the 'Cutty Sark'?

9. Who built the 'Great Western' steamship?

10. What is known as the 'Q.E.2.'?

11. Who sailed from Plymouth in the 'Mayflower' in 1620?

12. Who discovered the source of the Nile?

Art and Artists

Here's a mixture of questions about British artists and their works.

1. Who painted many famous pictures of the Suffolk countryside?

2. Which English painter has a special room in the Tate Gallery?

3. Was Edward Landseer most famous for his paintings of (a) animals (b) mountains, or (c) portraits?

4. Who painted 'Bubbles'?

5. Which 18th century painter was also a poet, famed for his 'Tiger, Tiger, Burning Bright' poem?

6. Who painted 'The Rake's Progress'?

7. Name one English pre-Raphaelite painter

8. Who painted 'Whistler's Mother'?

9. Which recent Prime Minister painted successfully for a hobby?

10. Who first illustrated Lewis Carroll's 'Alice in Wonderland'?

11. Which animal was George Stubbs famous for painting?

12. In which century did the painter Joshua Reynolds live?

Use the names of the pictured objects to fill in the gaps in the five incomplete place-names.

L	U						
		N	E	R			
	H		R	L		O	N
P	O	R	T	S			
C	H	E	L			H	A	M

1. What is the collective name for a group of partridges?

2. Name a reptile which is a native of Britain

3. Which is the most common of British birds?

4. Is the spider an insect?

5. What is a heifer?

6. Is a 'Natterjack' (a) a bird? (b) a toad? or (c) a water-rat?

7. Name an amphibian of the British Isles

8. Which of the following animals can still be found living wild in the British Isles: (a) wolf (b) elk? or (c) reindeer?

9. What is the collective name for a group of sheep?

10. Are moles blind?

11. In which English county would you find Chinese deer living wild?

12. How many species of land mammals are there in the British Isles: (a) 104? (b) 57? or (c) 21?

The Foot Game

Each of these descriptions, etc., should suggest a word or phrase containing the word 'foot'. Kick the game around and see how well you do.

1. An old English highwayman

2. Game played at Wembley stadium

3. Impression left in earth or snow

4. A disease of cows and pigs

5. At the front of the stage

6. A term used in boxing

7. A servant

8. To pay an account

9. Make a bad start

10. A term used in tennis

11. Trodden down

12. A reference at the bottom of a page

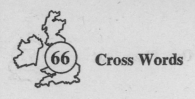

Here are six different British examples of the Christian cross.
Can you put the right names to them?

Canterbury, Passion, St. Andrews, Bezant, Anchor, Celtic.

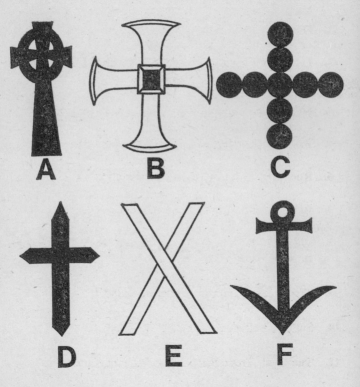

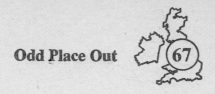

See if you can choose the place in each list that doesn't fit in with the others, and give the reason why.

1. Dartmoor, Plymouth, Exeter, Exmoor

2. Dublin, York, Epsom, Truro

3. Lake Windermere, Coniston Water, Lake Ullapool, Lake Ennerdale

4. Southampton, London, Birmingham, Liverpool

5. Brighton, Huddersfield, Blackpool, Southend

6. Rochdale, Grimsby, Salisbury, Bodmin

7. Bath, Taunton, Ipswich, Cheddar

8. White Hart Lane, Oxford Street, Stamford Bridge, Bramall Lane

9. Trowbridge, Kingston, Devizes, Swindon

10. Suffolk, Leicester, Dorset, Nottingham

11. The Oval, Trent Bridge, Twickenham, Lords

12. Manchester, Bolton, Bradford, Liverpool

Fact or Fiction?

Here's a handful of old English sayings and superstitions. Mark them True or False.

1. Lightning never strikes twice in the same place

2. Red sky at night, shepherd's delight

3. Nightingales only sing at night

4. Rain water is purer than tap water

5. No birds have teeth

6. Dogs can hear sounds we cannot hear

7. Brown eggs are more nourishing than white eggs

8. Dew falls

9. Once you've had the measles, you cannot have it again

10. A cold key on the back will help stop a nose-bleed

11. A person surfaces three times before drowning

12. Dragonflies sting

Monuments and Statues

1. Where is the Albert Memorial?

2. Are most statues made of: (a) iron? (b) plastic? or (c) granite?

3. What is the name of the statue in Piccadilly Circus?

4. Whose monument stands in Grosvenor Square?

5. Where is Nelson's Column?

6. Where is there a monument to Thomas Hardy?

7. In what county is there a statue of Captain Cook?

8. Where is there a memorial to the poet John Keats?

9. Who designed the lions at the foot of Nelson's column: (a) Inigo Jones? (b) Edward Landseer? or (c) John Constable?

10. In which part of Westminster Abbey are buried Shakespeare, Chaucer, Johnson, and other famous English writers?

11. Whose memorial stands at Loch Shiel, in Inverness-shire: (a) Robert Burns? or (b) Bonnie Prince Charlie?

12. Does the monument to the Great Fire of London stand near: (a) Pudding Lane? or (b) Buckingham Palace?

 **It's About Time**

Each of these descriptions, etc., should suggest a word or a phrase containing the word 'time'. See how many you can get right.

1. A proverb about delay and the ocean

2. The official world chronology

3. The weather vane at Lords cricket ground

4. Marching up and down on the spot

5. B.B.C. Radio's six pips

6. What publicans say when it's closing-time

7. How all good fairy tales begin

8. Repeatedly

9. A chronometer

10. Most factory workers have to use it

11. Extra work period

12. Old-fashioned

Can you work out just which county in Britain this girl comes from? Her face is made up of the letters in its name.

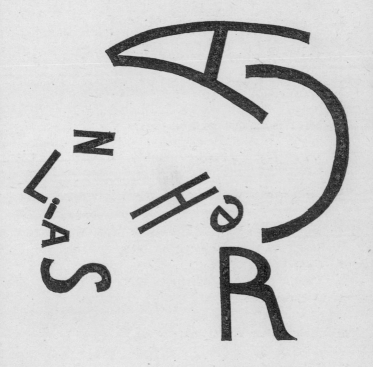

1. Which sports are associated with these places: (a) Twickenham? (b) Goodwood? (c) The Oval?

2. What is the correct length of a table tennis table?

3. Who was the last British men's singles tennis champion of Wimbledon?

4. Between which two points on the Thames is the Oxford v. Cambridge boat race held?

5. In which counties are these motor-circuits: (a) Silverstone? (b) Brands Hatch?

6. Where were the last Olympic Games in Britain held?

7. Where is the 'Derby' race held?

8. Which famous Victorian cricketer was also a village doctor?

9. What is the name of Chelsea's football ground?

10. Name the famous West Indian cricketer who played for Nottingham

11. In which counties are these horse-racing venues: (a) Ascot? (b) Sandown Park?

12. What is a 'googly' in cricket?

The Stone Game

Each of these descriptions, etc., should suggest a word or phrase containing the word 'stone'. See how many you can get right.

1. Found at the head of a grave

2. Neolithic monument on Salisbury Plain

3. First period of human culture

4. A gall-bladder impediment

5. An Irish monument one kisses

6. A royal keepsake hidden under a throne

7. A travelling bag

8. Shivering and not drunk

9. A semi-precious gem

10. Something very near

11. With no hearing

12. Make a thorough search

74   Cities and Towns

1. Name a city in England without a cathedral

2. Which city is famous for its old Roman watering-places?

3. In which counties are these towns: (a) Brighton? (b) Thetford?

4. Which is the smallest city in the British Isles?

5. Which are the most eastern and southern towns in the British Isles?

6. Name two cities in Yorkshire

7. Name a town in England that has a cathedral

8. Which is the largest town in the British Isles?

9. How many cities are there in the British Isles: (a) 60? (b) 45? or (c) 18?

10. Which are the most northern and western towns in the British Isles?

11. What are the two cities of London?

12. Name two cities in Hampshire

Fun with Phrases

Do you know what these everyday British phrases mean? Select the correct definitions.

1. To 'gild the lily'   (a) to make fun of (b) to make artificially beautiful

2. To 'kick the bucket'   (a) to sleep (b) to die

3. 'The lion's share'   (a) the largest part (b) the animal's portion

4. To 'bury the hatchet'   (a) to make work (b) to make peace

5. 'A pig in a poke'   (a) a bargain (b) something of unknown value

6. 'A mare's nest'   (a) a stupid belief (b) a great love

7. 'Job's comforter'   (a) one who hurts whilst comforting (b) a good priest

8. 'Crocodile tears'   (a) loud comment (b) false sorrow

9. To cry 'Wolf!'   (a) to give a false alarm (b) to frighten

10. 'Hobson's choice'   (a) a choice with no alternative (b) first choice

11. An 'Achilles' heel'   (a) a concealed weapon (b) a weak point

12. To 'tilt at windmills'   (a) to fight imaginary foes (b) to do useless things

76 Name the Rivers

Can you locate these 10 British rivers?

Thames, Cam, Forth, Mersey, Fal, Wey, Ouse, Trent, Wye, Tweed.

Kings and Queens

1. Which English King had six wives?

2. What are the first Christian names of the present Queen's four children?

3. Which two English kings were killed by stray arrows in battle?

4. What was the date of Queen Elizabeth II's accession to the throne?

5. Name an English sovereign who was born abroad

6. Where is Elizabeth I buried?

7. Who is the present Prince of Wales?

8. Which Queen said, 'We are not amused'?

9. Which king abdicated to marry an American woman?

10. How did Lady Jane Grey die?

11. Which Scottish king is said to have learned the art of patience from a spider?

12. Who is married to Princess Margaret?

Pop Puzzles

Can you pick the one British pop singer out of each of the following groups?

1. Sarah Vaughan, Dusty Springfield, Diana Ross

2. Elvis Presley, Rick Nelson, Cliff Richard

3. Ella Fitzgerald, Doris Day, Lulu

4. George Melly, Ed Thigpen, Country Joe

5. Frankie Laine, David Bowie, Guy Mitchell

6. Tommy Steele, David Cassidy, Paul Simon

7. Anita Harris, Anita O'Day, Janis Joplin

8. Art Garfunkel, Tom Jones, King Pleasure

9. Mick Jagger, Bob Dylan, Slim Whitman

10. Marty Wilde, Joe Williams, Tennessee Ernie Ford

11. Andy Williams, Perry Como, Marc Bolan

12. Johnny Cash, Donny Osmond, Donovan

Starting with the 'U' and the 'US' at the top, can you make a word on each of the other four lines by adding one new letter each time to those you already have? (The silhouette of the game bird is a clue for the last word.)

80 County By County

1. How many counties are there in England and Wales: (a) 99? (b) 76? or (c) 55?

2. Which is the largest county in England?

3. Name an English county which has been split into East and West divisions

4. In which county is the Cheddar Gorge?

5. Which is the largest county in Scotland?

6. Which English county is bounded by only one other county?

7. In which county is incorporated the Isle of Ely?

8. Where is the county of Tipperary?

9. Which is the smallest county in England?

10. Which county ceased to exist in 1962, though its name is still used?

11. How many counties are there in Ulster?

12. How many counties is Gloucestershire bounded by: (a) 2? (b) 4? or (c) 8?

Weather Forecast

1. What is usually the wettest month in Britain?

2. What is usually the driest month in Britain?

3. Which is the wettest area in the British Isles?

4. Which is the driest area in the British Isles?

5. What city in England is traditionally associated with rain?

6. How many colours in a rainbow, and what are they?

7. Is the saying 'March comes in like a lion and goes out like a lamb' usually true or false?

8. What is the name for a wind over 73 m.p.h.?

9. When does mist technically become fog?

10. What is the 'Beaufort Scale'?

11. What is snow?

12. What is the name given to frozen dew?

82 British Allsorts

1. Who owns Longleat House?

2. Which three counties of England roughly form 'The Weald'?

3. Where is the 'Derby' horse race held?

4. In which county is the Cheddar Gorge?

5. Which of these film stars were born in England: Charlie Chaplin, Cary Grant, Bob Hope?

6. What is the Welsh National Eisteddfod?

7. In what year did the General Strike take place?

8. What colours do the Ireland football team wear?

9. What happened to the liner 'Titanic' in 1912?

10. What is the Scottish village of John O' Groats famous for?

11. In which county is Bodmin Moor?

12. What were the famous last words of Admiral Lord Nelson?

Coast to Coast

1. At which seaside resort would you find Madame Taussaud's Waxworks?

2. Which town has the longest pier—Blackpool or Southend?

3. Where is Beachy Head?

4. Where is Dodman Point?

5. Near what seaside city would you find Eddystone Lighthouse?

6. Which famous English seaside resort has as its main attraction a large copy of Paris's Eiffel Tower?

7. How tall are the highest cliffs in England: (a) 400ft? (b) 900ft? or (c) 1200ft?

8. At which seaside resort would you find the 'Golden Mile'?

9. Which is the nearest county to the Isle of Wight?

10. In which Welsh county is the Gower Peninsula?

11. Cornwall has the longest coastline in Great Britain. How long is it: (a) 174 miles? (b) 205 miles? or (c) 321 miles?

12. Which is said to be the most dangerous spot in English coastal waters?

Sporting Scribble

Can you turn the squiggly lines below into the names of four popular British sports, simply by adding 18 straight lines?

> Dcrts

> locieu

> Dolo

> Digdu

How Well Do You Know Wales?

1. Which city is near Barry Island?

2. Is the leek the Welsh national emblem?

3. How many counties are there in Wales?

4. What is Offa's Dyke?

5. Name two football league clubs that have their grounds in Wales

6. What is 'Fishguard'?

7. Is the chief mineral mined in Wales (a) coal? (b) iron? or (c) tin?

8. In which century was the first Prince of Wales created?

9. What musical instrument is associated with Wales?

10. Where is St David's University College?

11. In which century was Wales brought under English law?

12. What is the county town of Pembroke?

Here's a batch of old English proverbs, very much over-written. See if you can work out what the proverbs are.

1. A mass of concreted earthy material perenially rotating on its axis will not accumulate an accretion of byro-phyric vegetation.

2. Do not dissipate your competence by hebetudinous prodigality lest you subsequently lament an exiguous in-adequacy.

3. Too many people skilled in the preparation of gastro-nomic concoctions will impair the quality of a certain potable solution.

4. That prudent avis which matutinally deserts its abode will ensnare a vermiculate creature.

5. It is a maleficient horizontally-propelled current of gaseous matter whose portentous advent is not the har-binger of a modicum of beneficence.

6. Everything that coruscates with effulgence is not a soft precious metal.

Here is a selection of singular nouns. See how many you can pluralise properly.

1.	Mouse	13.	Moss
2.	Ox	14.	Louse
3.	Lullaby	15.	Lighthouse
4.	Mosquito	16.	Bye
5.	Valley	17.	Cockney
6.	Sheaf	18	Die
7.	Echo	19.	Folio
8.	Reindeer	20.	Rain
9.	Titmouse	21.	Loaf
10.	Owl	22.	Englishman
11.	Gallows	23.	Gladiolus
12.	Armful	24.	Quiz

1. Where is the F.A. Cup Final held?

2. What festival is Nottingham famous for?

3. What is the route of the yearly Veteran Car Run?

4. In what Cornish town does the 'Floral Dance' take place?

5. Where in London does the 'Trooping the Colour' take place?

6. What is the biggest dog show in Great Britain called?

7. Who get the first prize in the Dunmow Flitch Trial?

8. During which month is the Motor Show usually held?

9. What food do you usually associate with Shrove Tuesday?

10. In which city is the Lord Mayor's Show held?

11. On which of the Channel Islands does the 'Battle of the Flowers' take place?

12. What two teams compete in the annual Boat Race on the Thames?

Garden Games

The names of three popular British flowers are hidden in these columns of letters. See if you can find them by taking one letter from each row in turn, working from top to bottom. All the letters must be used, but none more than once. The three flowers are shown in the drawing.

N	P	D
E	A	O
S	L	L
P	Y	T
H	U	A
R	I	N
T	T	N
I	H	I
U	U	U
M	S	M

1. Who wrote the novel 'A Tale of Two Cities'?

2. What kind of book is 'Hansard'?

3. Which book published has sold the most copies?

4. Name the titles of two plays written by Oscar Wilde

5. To which English library must a free copy of every new book published be sent?

6. Who was the first Englishman to print books?

7. Who wrote the novel 'War of the Worlds'?

8. What kind of book is 'Wisden'?

9. On which play by George Bernard Shaw was the film 'My Fair Lady' based?

10. Which famous family of Victorian sisters all wrote books?

11. Who wrote 'The Decline and Fall of the Roman Empire'?

12. Which poet wrote the lines:

    "Grow along old with me,
    The best is yet to be."

All of these are nicknames for famous British people, land-marks, etc.—past and present. Can you give their real names?

1. 'The Iron Duke'

2. 'Big Ben'

3. 'The Chelsea Pensioners'

4. 'The Old Lady of Threadneedle Street'

5. 'The Bard of Avon'

6. 'Tin Pan Alley'

7. 'The Virgin Queen'

8. 'The Gunners'

9. 'The Emerald Isle'

10. 'The Demon Barber'

11. 'The Man of a Thousand Disguises'

12. 'The Delectable Duchy'

92 Topsy-Turvy Rivers

If you collect each group of letters together—there are four groups—and arrange them correctly, you'll find the names of four British rivers.

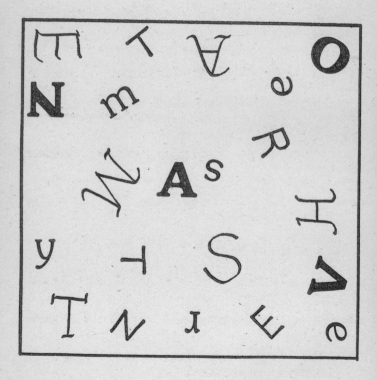

Punny Business

Try and fill in the blanks in these sentences. The word after the missing word has the same sound, but a different spelling and meaning.

1. I love the banks and ——— (*brays*) of bonnie Scotland

2. The ——— (*row*) deer fled into the New Forest

3. The ——— (*wreak*) of fish at Billingsgate market is awful

4. Many witches were burned at the ——— (*steak*) in 16th century England

5. A lot of ——— (*swayed*) shoes are made in England

6. The queen wore a dress of delicate ——— (*tool*)

7. An Elizabethan dandy used to wear a ——— (*rough*) around his neck

8. Welsh choirs are noted for their beautiful ——— (*him*) singing

9. There are many ——— (*prince*) by Constable for sale in the Tate Gallery

10. The best place to grow ——— (*flocks*) is Southern England

11. There isn't much sand on the ——— (*beech*) at Brighton ; mainly pebbles

12. Little Miss Muffet ate her curds and ——— (*way*)

D

Pick the Place

Match these famous people with their birthplaces.

1.	William Shakespeare	(a)	*Dublin*
2.	Bob Hope	(b)	*Kensington Palace, London*
3.	Oliver Cromwell	(c)	*Max Gate, Dorset*
4.	Thomas Hardy	(d)	*Huntingdon*
5.	Queen Victoria	(e)	*Stratford-on-Avon*
6.	Jonathan Swift	(f)	*Eltham, London*
7.	Dr Livingstone	(g)	*Bruton Street, London*
8.	Charlie Chaplin	(h)	*Alloway, Ayrshire*
9.	Robert Burns	(i)	*Blenheim Palace*
10.	Winston Churchill	(j)	*Walworth, London*
11.	Queen Elizabeth II	(k)	*Burnham Thorpe, Norfolk*
12.	Lord Nelson	(l)	*Blantyre, Lanark*

See if you can re-arrange the letters on each of these signs, and find out to which towns or cities in Britain they point.

Fradfic   8

Rock   6

Bludin   5

Prowten   1

Which British singers (or groups) had big hits with these songs?

1. 'With a Little Help from My Friends'

2. 'Pin-ups'

3. 'Living Doll'

4. 'Liverpool Lou'

5. 'Rock Me Baby'

6. 'Celebrity Ball'

7. 'Delilah'

8. 'Wouldn't It Be Luverly?'

9. 'Move It'

10. 'Country Comfort'

11. 'Blockbuster'

12. 'Big Spender'

Can you match these twelve towns with their correct counties?

1. Grimsby   (a) *Berkshire*

2. Salisbury   (b) *Dorset*

3. Dover   (c) *Somerset*

4. Godalming   (d) *Hampshire*

5. Camborne   (e) *Lincolnshire*

6. Sunderland   (f) *Surrey*

7. Stratford-on-Avon   (g) *Devon*

8. Reading   (h) *Cornwall*

9. Andover   (i) *Durham*

10. Yeovil   (j) *Warwickshire*

11. Dorchester   (k) *Wiltshire*

12. Torquay   (l) *Kent*

What Are You Eating?

See if you can choose an accurate description of these British foods from the choice given:

1. Tripe comes from a cow's kidneys / lungs / stomach

2. The main ingredient of baking powder is aspirin / yeast / bicarbonate of soda

3. Brisket of beef refers to meat from a calf / a cut of beef / a size of joint

4. Pigs' trotters are pigs' ears/feet/noses

5. A Welsh rarebit is grilled cheese on toast/stewed/hare/ broiled venison

6. Dumplings are served with salad/peaches/stew

7. Corned beef is beef that has been slow-baked / cooked in corn / pickled in brine

8. Tapioca is a cereal/starch/fruit

9. Faggots are made mostly of liver / flour / potatoes

10. Dill is a herb / fruit / oil

11. Braised meat has been cooked then baked / pounded heavily / stewed

12. Haggis consists mainly of pheasant / offal / pork

Here are six leaves that can be seen in the British countryside. Can you identify them?

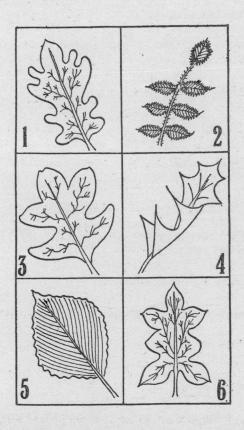

1. What is a 'gazebo'?

2. What is the name given to a single upright stone erected in Neolithic times?

3. What colour is a Hereford cow?

4. What are 'follies'?

5. Were windmills introduced into England in (a) 1182? (b) 1521? or (c) 1910?

6. What is the origin of most public parks?

7. What is a 'ha-ha'?

8. When was cock-fighting made illegal: (a) 1711? (b) 1835? or (c) 1970?

9. What was a 'quintain'?

10. Is a 'brock' (a) a pigsty? (b) a tall tower? or (c) a hedge trimmer?

11. What is the most popular animal depicted in the chalk drawings of Wiltshire?

12. Could you climb over a 'crinkle-crankle'?

Answers

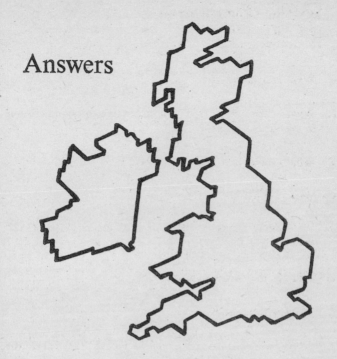

Answers

1. A. Perthshire. B. Devon. C. Sussex. D. Wiltshire. E. Northampton. F. Suffolk. G. Yorkshire. H. Herefordshire.

2. 1. London Bridge. 2. Saltash, Cornwall. 3. b. 4. The London Underground system (6 miles). 5. Isambard Kingdom Brunel. 6. Tower Bridge. 7. Underneath the Thames in east London. 8. Ironbridge. The others are in Cornwall. 9. a. 10. Wood. 11. The Tay Bridge. 12. Fulham.

3. 1. Oxonian. 2. Liverpudlian. 3. Heliogonian. 4. Mancunian 5. Londoner. 6. Devonian. 7. Welshman. 8 Aberdonian. 9. Cantabrigian. 10. Manxman. 11. Dubliner. 12. Glaswegian.

4. 1. The Shannon: 240 miles. 2. The Thames. 3. The Dee. 4. London and Birmingham. 5. a. 6. Staffordshire. 7. No; it is a lake. 8. a. 9. The Stour. 10. The Derwent. 11. (a) Thames, (b) Humber. 12. b.

5. Churchill.

6. 1. The British Museum. 2. b. 3. London. 4. In the National Gallery. 5. The Natural History Museum. 6. The Tate Gallery. 7. Fleet Street. 8. Ship's figureheads. 9. a. 10. The Kensington Museum. 11. On the Isle of Man. 12. Madame Tussaud's, London.

7. 1. Lollipop (Cloud). 2. Deckchair (Joy). 3. Frog (Day). 4. Gherkins (Ways). 5. Omnibus (Night). 6. Grandfather (Church). 7. Knees (Feet). 8. Drunkard (Curfew). 9. Trousers (Head). 10. Pomegranate (Rose). 11. Refrigerator (Garden). 12. Ears (Eyes).

8. 1. Marylebone Cricket Club. 2. Queen's Counsel. 3. Bachelor of Arts. 4. His (or Her) Royal Highness. 5. Absent Without Leave. 6. Football Association. 7. Royal Society for the Prevention of Cruelty to Animals. Member of Parliament. 9. Royal Academician. 10. On Her Majesty's Service. 11. Member of the British Empire. 12. Lawn Tennis Association.

9. Guildford. Sheffield. Glasgow. Ipswich.

10. 1. Tipperary. 2. Glasgow. 3. Londoner. 4. Man. 5. Finchley. 6. Blaydon. 7. Sussex 8 Winchester 9. Eton. 10. Wimbledon. 11. Liverpool. 12. Tralee.

11. 1. b. 2. Isle of Wight. 3. b; it doesn't exist. 4. Jersey, Guernsey, Sark, Alderney. 5. St. Michael's Mount. 6. A dockland on the North bank of the Thames. 7. Between the Orkneys and the Shetlands. 8. The tail-less cat. 9. a. 10. Yes. 11. In Kent. 12. The Atlantic.

12. In Ross-shire 2050ft. 2. Modern road surfacing. 3. London and Leeds. 4. 280 miles. 5. b. 6. A route for cattle. 7. No. 8. Roads with a toll-gate. 9. 370 miles. 10. a. 11. No: the speed limit was 14 m.p.h. 12. Only by the same way you went in.

13. 'Many Hands Make Light Work.'

14. 1. Real. 2. c. 3. 'The Canterbury Tales'. 4. King John. 5. The Black Death. 6. King Harold. 7. b. 8. King Alfred the Great. 9. Leader of the Peasants' Revolt in 1450. 10. Winchester. 11. William Langland. 12. King Canute.

15. 1. Medical consultants. 2. Highgate Cemetery. 3. The British Museum. (The biggest is in the Vatican, Rome.) 4. The Collegiate Church of St. Peter. 5. Twickenham. 6. Tailors. 7. On the Thames Embankment. 8. c. 9. Lord's. 10. South Kensington. 11. The Bow Street Runners. 12. Baker Street.

16. 1. d. 2. h. 3. g. 4. i. 5. j. 6. a. 7. 1. 8. k. 9. e. 10. c. 11. b. 12. f.

17. 1. True. 2. True. 3. True. 4. True. 5. False. 6. False. 7 True. 8. False. 9. False. 10. False. 11. True. 12. False.

18. Swallow. Nitwit. Robin Hood. Swanage.

19. 1. Sullivan. 2. Tweedledee. 3. Isolde. 4. Circumstance. 5. Mr. Hyde. 6. Soda. 7. Watson. 8. Judy. 9. Guinevere. 10. Jill. 11. Allen. 12. Joan.

20. 1. Mash. 2. Yorkshire pudding. 3. Chips. 4. Custard. 5. Carrots. 6. Cream. 7. Onions. 8. Pickles. 9. Eggs. 10. Squeak. 11. Marmalade. 12. Dumplings.

21. A. Cornwall. B. Norfolk. C. Hampshire. D. Dorset.

22. 1. Its 'Kissing Stone'. 2. Pembrokeshire. 3. Stone, Bronze and Iron. 4. In the gatehouse. 5. The largest artificial earth mound in Europe. 6. Windsor Castle. 7. Framlingham, Suffolk. 8. Tintagel. 9. The remains of an Iron Age village. 10. Windsor: all the others are in Wales. 11. Doune, Perthshire. 12. The main tower.

23. 1. Black Death. 2. Black Beauty. 3. Black sheep. 4. Black and Tans. 5. The Black Watch. 6. Black Maria. 7. Black-Bottom. 8. Black market. 9. Blackbeard. 10. Blackbird. 11. Black look. 12. Black-out.

24. 1. Hen party. 2. Gay dog. 3. Road hog. 4. Early bird. 5. Cat burglar. 6. Shrimp. 7. Sitting duck. 8. Black sheep. 9. Work horse. 10. Night owl. 11. Sour-puss. 12. Greedy pig.

25. 1. a. 2. a. 3. b. 4. a. 5. c. 6. a. 7. b. 8. c. 9. b. 10. b. 11. b. 12. a.

26. Pride Comes Before a Fall.

27. 1. White Paper. 2. 'The Woman in White.' 3. Whitehall. 4. The White Knight. 5. Little white lie. 6. The white feather (or flag). 7. Whitechapel. 8. White Hart Lane. 9. White pine. 10. White man's burden. 11. Whitewash. 12. White elephant.

28. 1. Scafell Pike: 3,210ft. 2. In the North Riding of Yorkshire. 3. Stirlingshire. 4. Snowdon, Snaefell. 5. Snowdon: 3,560ft. 6. A series of chalk cliffs near Eastbourne, Sussex. 7. Northumberland. 8. b. 9. Carrauntoohil: 3,414ft. 10. Ben Nevis—the others are in the Lake District. 11. Ben Nevis: 4,406ft. 12. Surrey.

29. 1. West Sussex. 2. Portsmouth. 3. Cornish. Yorkshire. 4. Bryher, St. Agnes, St. Martin's, St. Mary's and Tresco. 5. Canterbury—all the others are county towns. 6. Lancashire. 7. Between Southampton and the Isle of Wight. 8. Liverpool. 9. c. 10. They are all sites of BBC transmission stations. 11. In Norfolk, Lincolnshire, and Cambridge. 12. North Yorkshire.

30. Start on the central 'E' and find: eagle, tit, robin, heron, swallow.

31. 1. Horsted Park, Sussex. 2. a. 3. Clapham Junction. 4. George Stephenson. 5. The Fleet Line. 6. The Tay Bridge, Dundee—two miles long. 7. Southwark. 8.

Southern, Western, Eastern, North-Eastern, Scottish, London-Midland. 9. Isambard Kingdom Brunel. 10. Camborne, Cornwall, to Wick, Caithness. 11. c. 12. St. Pancras.

32. Being the most northerly part of the mainland. 2. Glasgow. 3. A fur pouch worn in the front of a kilt. 4. A 16th century church reformer and historian. 5. Invernessshire. 6. b. 7. Hampden Park. 8. The royal castle. 9. Angus. 10. Yes. 11. A Jacobite heroine who helped Bonnie Prince Charlie to escape from George I's army. 12. The bagpipes.

33. 1. Lincoln green. 2. Gretna Green. 3. Greengage. 4. Graham Greene. 5. Green Park. 6. Greengrocer. 7. green-eyed monster. 8. 'The Wearing of the Green', 'Forty Shades of Green'. 9. A green thumb (or green fingers). 10. The grass is always greener. 11. 'Greensleeves'. 12. 'Green Grow the Rushes-O'.

34. Eons, nest, norse, nose, note, notes, open, ores, pens, pent, peon, pert, person, pest, pets, prone, prose, pore, pores, post, pots, rent, rents, rest, rope, ropes, sent, snore, snort, sort, spent, spore, sport, spot, step, stone, store, stop, tern, tone, tones, tons, tore, torn.

35. 1. The Blue Lamp. 2. Bluestocking. 3. Blueprints. 4. 'The Bluebells of Scotland'. 5. Little Boy Blue. 6. Once in a blue moon. 7. Blue-blooded. 8. Blue-pencil. 9. To blue money. 10. Blue Ribbon. 11. 'The Sky-Blues'. 12. Boys In Blue.

36. 1. Westminster, London. 2. Conservative, Labour, Liberal. 3. Harold Macmillan. 4. Yes. 5. Balls Pond Road. 6. All of them, except clergymen. 7. 10 Downing Street, London SW1. 8. Chequers. 9. b. 10. Heath, Wilson and Thorpe. 11. 5 years. 12. Baldwin – five times.

37. 1. Richmal Crompton. 2. William Shakespeare. 3. J. R. R. Tolkein. 4. Sir Arthur Conan Doyle. 5. Ian Fleming. 6. Charles Dickens. 7. Lewis Carroll. 8. Thomas Hardy. 9. Kenneth Grahame. 10. A. J. Cronin. 11. Somerset Maugham. 12. P. G. Wodehouse.

38. 1. Yes. 2. Yes. 3. No—in America. 4. Yes. 5. No—in America. 6. Yes. 7. Yes. 8. No—in Greece. 9. No—in America. 10. Yes. 11. No—in China. 12. No—in France.

39. Snowdon, Ben Nevis, Cambrian, Skiddaw.

40. 1. Birch: the others are evergreen trees. 2. An organism devoid of chlorophyll, reproduced by spores. 3. Hampshire. 4. Yes. 5. Hawthorn, Rowan, Apple, Quince, Plum, Pear. 6. Willow. 7. Poppy. 8. Woodbine. 9. Bluebell: the others belong to the pea family. 10. Gloucestershire. 11. Yew. 12. Chile Pine.

41. 1. Little Red Riding Hood. 2. Red Cross. 3. Red nose. 4. Red herring. 5. Redcoat. 6. 'The Red-Headed League'. 7. Redbreast. 8. Red-letter day. 9. To lay out the red carpet. 10. Red light. 11. Red tape. 12. Red-handed.

42. 1. Blackpool. 2. Penzance. 3. Brighton. 4. Southend.

43. 1. Dublin. 2. c. 3. Leinster, Munster, Ulster, Connaught. 4. Kerry. 5. Green. 6. The Shamrock. 7. Northern. 8. b. 9. Fermanagh. 10. Belfast. 11. b. 12. Belfast.

44. 1. Old St. Paul's, London: 520ft. high. 2. Bell-metal, a kind of bronze. 3. Sir Christopher Wren. 4. The Roman Catholic, Liverpool Metropolitan cathedral, consecrated in 1967. 5. A covered gate at the entrance to a church. 6. a. 7. Someone born within the sound of 'Bow Bells', in Cheapside. 8. 2. 9. Truro, Lichfield. 10. Westminster Abbey. 11. 'Great St. Paul', in St. Paul's: it weighs 16¾ tons. 12. Salisbury.

45. Bristol. Hull. York. Bath.

46. 1. Black and white stripes. 2. Claret, with light blue sleeves. 3. Red and white stripes. 4. Red, with white sleeves. 5. Blue. 6. Green and white hoops. 7. Red. 8. Blue and white quarters. 9. Red and black stripes. 10. Yellow. 11. White. 12. Blue and white stripes.

47. 1. True. 2. True. 3. False. 4. True. 5. False. 6. True. 7. True. 8. False. 9. True. 10. False. 11. False. 12. True.

48. 1. Hindhead, Surrey. 2. They are all headlands on the Welsh coast. 3. The Giant's Causeway. 4. Guildford, Surrey. 5. A fiord. 6. Sussex. 7. A 'U' shape, steep sides, morainic debris. 8. Richmond Park. 9. Cornwall. 10. Dunmail: the others are Lake District peaks. 11. b. 12. In the Orkneys.

49. 1. f. 2. i. 3. g. 4. k. 5. b. 6. d. 7. e. 8. a. 9. j. 10. h. 11. l. 12. c.

50. 1. John Keats. 2. Winston Churchill. 3. Alexander Pope. 4. Lord Nelson. 5. Harold Macmillan. 6. Lord Tennyson. 7. Samuel Johnson. 8. Rudyard Kipling. 9. Lord Chesterfield. 10. Rupert Brooke.

51. Deal. Durham.

52. 1. False. 2. False. 3. False. 4. True. 5. True. 6. True 7. True. 8. False. 9. False. 10. True. 11. False. 12. True.

53. 1. Belfast. 2. Steel. 3. Yorkshire. 4. Yorkshire. 5. Sunny and rainy. 6. Eastern England. 7. Jute: it is imported. 8. Black and white. 9. Barley, wheat and oats. 10. Port Talbot, Wales. 11. Tin. 12. Motors.

54. 1. b. 2. c. 3. c. 4. a. 5. b. 6. c. 7. a. 8. b. 9. c. 10. b. 11. b. 12. a.

55. 1. Harwich. 2. All were once big ports, but are no longer used. 3. Plymouth. 4. c. 5. No vehicles are allowed on them, for they are too steep. 6. London. 7. Rye, Winchester, Dover, Hythe, Hastings, Romney. 8. Newcastle. 9. Whitby: the others are ports. 10. Fishguard, Holyhead, Liverpool, Stranraer, Glasgow, Preston. 11. b. 12. Newport.

56. Leeds. Epsom. Truro.

57. 1. Yes (in the 18th century). 2. Somerset. 3. Thistle. 4. No. 5. London Airport (Heathrow). 6. 10 million. 7. Wimbledon. 8. Brendan Behan. 9. George VI. 10. Yes. 11. Yes. 12. 625 lines.

58. 1. 1970. 2. 240. 3. 10p. 4. 5p. 5. £1.05. 6. Blue. 7. Silver. 8. Eight. 9. Brown. 10. The Chief Cashier of the Bank of England. 11. Five shillings. 12. £25.

59. Eel. Perch. Bream. Mackerel.

60. Brighton. 2. London. 3. Edinburgh. 4. Nottingham. 5. Glasgow. 6. London. 7. Land's End. 8. Cardiff. 9. London. 10. Buckfastleigh. 11. London. 12. Swindon.

61. 1. Sir Francis Drake. 2. The English Channel. 3. Captain James Cook. 4. Victoria Falls. 5. a. 6. Gas and oil. 7. Fathoms (6ft. lengths). 8. A clipper. 9. Isambard Kingdom Brunel. 10. The liner Queen Elizabeth II. 11. The Pilgrim Fathers. 12. John Speke.

62. 1. John Constable. 2. James Turner. 3. a. 4. John Millais. 5. William Blake. 6. William Hogarth. 7. Rossetti, Millais, Morris, Burne-Jones. 8. James McNeill Whistler. 9. Winston Churchill. 10. John Tenniel. 11. The horse. 12. 18th.

63. Luton, Pinner. Charlton. Portsmouth. Cheltenham.

64. 1. Covey. 2. Grass snake, adder, common lizard, slow-worm. 3. The blackbird. 4. No, it is an arachnid. 5. A young cow. 6. b. 7. Newt, toad, frog. 8. c. Flock. 10. No. 11. Bedfordshire (at Whitchurch). 12. b.

65. 1. Footpad. 2. Football. 3. Footprint. 4. Foot and mouth disease. 5. Footlights. 6. Footwork. 7. Footman. 8. Foot the bill. 9. Get off on the wrong foot. 10. Foot-fault. 11. Underfoot. 12. Footnote.

66. A. Celtic. B. Canterbury. C. Bezant. D. Passion. E. St. Andrews. F. Anchor.

67. 1. Exmoor: the rest are in Devon. 2. Epsom: all the others are cities. 3. Ullapool: the others are in the Lake District. 4. Birmingham: the others have docks. 5. Huddersfield: all the others are by the sea. 6. Salisbury: the others are towns. 7. Ipswich: the rest are in Somerset. 8. Oxford Street: the others are football grounds. 9. Kingston: the others are in Wiltshire. 10. Leicester: all the others are counties. 11. Twickenham: the others are cricket grounds. 12. Bradford: the rest are in Lancashire.

68. 1. False. 2. True. 3. False. 4. False. 5. True. 6. True. 7. False. 8. False. 9. True. 10. False. 11. False. 12. False.

69. 1. Kensington Gardens. 2. c. 3. Eros. 4. Franklin D. Roosevelt. 5. Trafalgar Square. 6. Portesham, Dorset. 7. Yorkshire. 8. In Keat's Place, Hampstead. 9. b. 10. Poet's Corner. 11. b. 12. a.

70. 1. Time and tide wait for no man. 2. Greenwich Mean Time. 3. Father Time. 4. Marking time. 5. Time signal. 6. 'Time, gentlemen, please'. 7. 'Once upon a time . . .' 8. Time and time again. 9. Timepiece. 10. Time-clock. Overtime. 12. Behind the times.

71. Lancashire.

72. 1. (a) Rugby. (b) Horse-racing. (c) Cricket. 2. 9ft. x 5ft. 3. Fred Perry, in 1936. 4. Putney and Mortlake. 5. (a) Northants. (b) Kent. 6. Wembley, in 1948. 7. Epsom, in Surrey. 8. W. G. Grace. 9. Stamford Bridge. 10. Sir Gary Sobers. 11. (a) Berkshire. (b) Surrey. 12. A slow type of bowling delivery.

73. 1. Tombstone. 2. Stonehenge. 3. The Stone Age. 4. Gallstone. 5. The Blarney Stone. 6. The Coronation Stone (the Stone of Scone). 7. Gladstone. 8. Stone cold sober. Moonstone, bloodstone, sunstone. 10. Within a stone's throw. 11. Stone deaf. 12. Leave no stone unturned.

74. 1.Hull, Stoke, Nottingham. 2. Bath. 3. (a) Sussex. (b) Norfolk. 4. Wells. 5. Lowestoft, Suffolk; Helston, Cornwall. 6. Bradford, Hull, Leeds, Sheffield, York. 7. Derby, Guildford, Blackburn, Southwell. 8. Sunderland. 9. (a). 10. Lerwick, Shetland; Dingle, Kerry. 11. City of London; City of Westminster. 12. Winchester; Southampton.

75. 1. b. 2. b. 3. a. 4. b. 5. b. 6. a. 7. a. 8. b. 10. a. 11. b. 12. a.

76. A. Cam. B. Fal. C. Wye. D. Ouse. E. Mersey. F. Forth. G. Tweed. H. Trent. I. Wey. J. Thames.

77. 1. Henry VIII. 2. Charles, Anne, Andrew, Edward. 3. Harold and Richard I. 4. 6th February, 1952. 5. William I and II, Henry II, George I and II. 6. Westminster Abbey. 7. Prince Charles. 8. Queen Victoria. 9. Edward VIII (Duke of Windsor). 10. She was beheaded at the Tower of London. 11. Robert I, the Bruce. 12. Lord Snowdon.

78. 1. Dusty Springfield. 2. Cliff Richard. 3. Lulu. 4. George Melly. 5. David Bowie. 6. Tommy Steele. 7. Anita Harris. 8. Tom Jones. 9. Mick Jagger. 10. Marty Wilde. 11. Marc Bolan. 12. Donovan.

79. U, Us, Use, Ruse, Rouse, Grouse.

80. 1. c. 2. North Yorkshire. 3. Sussex. 4. Somerset. 5. Inverness-shire. 6. Cornwall. 7. Cambridgeshire. 8. Eire. 9. The Isle of Wight. 10. Middlesex. 11. Six. 12. c.

81. 1. October. 2. April. 3. The Lake District. 4. Essex and Kent. 5. Manchester. 6. Seven: red, orange, yellow, green, blue, indigo and violet. 7. False. 8. A hurricane. 9. When visibility is less than 1,000 yards. 10. A table for measuring the strength of winds. 11. Ice crystals formed from water vapour at below-freezing temperature. 12. Hoar frost.

82. 1. The Marquess of Bath. 2. Surrey, Sussex and Kent. 3. At Epsom, in Surrey. 4. Somerset. 5. All of them were. 6. An annual gathering of musicians and poets. 7. 1926. 8. Green shirts, white shorts. 9. It sank, on its first voyage. 10. It is the most northerly town in Britain. 11. Cornwall. 12. 'Kiss me, Hardy.'

83. 1. Brighton. 2. At Southend: the pier is $1\frac{1}{3}$ miles long. 3. East Sussex. 4. Off the Cornish coast. 5. Plymouth. 6. Blackpool. 7. (c)—900ft. The Countisbury Cliffs in Devon. 8. Blackpool. 9. Hampshire. 10. Glamorganshire. c. 12. The Goodwin Sands.

84. Darts. Hockey. Polo. Rugby.

85. 1. Cardiff. 2. No—the daffodil is. 3. Six. 4. A great earthwork created by King Offa. 5. Cardiff, Swansea, Wrexham, Newport. 6. A fishing port in Pembrokeshire. 7. a. 8. 14th. 9. Harp. 10. Lampeter. 11. 16th. 12. Haverfordwest.

86. 1. A rolling stone gathers no moss. 2. Waste not, want not. 3. Too many cooks spoil the broth. 4. The early bird catches the worm. 5. It's an ill wind that blows nobody any good. 6. All that glisters is not gold.

87. 1. Mice. 2. Oxen. 3. Lullabies. 4. Mosquitoes. 5. Valleys. 6. Sheaves. 7. Echoes. 8. Reindeer. 9. Titmice. 10. Owls. 11. Gallowses. 12. Armfuls. 13. Mosses. 14. Lice. 15. Lighthouses. 16. Byes. 17. Cockneys. 18. Dice. 19. Folios. 20. Rains. 21. Loaves. 22. Englishmen. 23. Gladioli. 24. Quizzes.

88. 1. Wembley Stadium. 2. The Goose Fair. 3. London to Brighton. 4. Helston. 5. Horse Guards Parade. 6. Cruft's Dog Show. 7. The most happily married couple. 8. October. 9. Pancakes. 10. London. 11. Jersey. 12. Oxford and Cambridge.

89. Nasturtium. Polyanthus. Delphinium.

90. 1. Charles Dickens. 2. A report of parliamentary debates. 3. The Bible. 4. 'Lady Windermere's Fan', 'The Importance of Being Earnest', 'Salome', 'A Woman of No Importance', 'An Ideal Husband'. 5. The British Museum. 6. William Caxton, in 1473. H. G. Wells. 8. A yearly cricket annual. 9. 'Pygmalion'. 10. The Brontës: Charlotte, Emily and Anne. 11. Edward Gibbon. 12. Robert Browning.

91. 1. The Duke of Wellington. 2. The bell in Parliament Tower. 3. Chelsea football team. 4. The Bank of England. 5. William Shakespeare. 6. London's music-publishing area. 7. Queen Elizabeth I. 8. Arsenal football team. 9. Ireland. 10. Sweeney Todd. 11. Sherlock Holmes. 12. Cornwall.

92. Avon. Thames. Mersey. Trent.

93. 1. Braes. 2. Roe. 3. Reek. 4. Stake. 5. Suede. 6. Tulle. 7. Ruff. 8. Hymn. 9. Prints. 10. Phlox. 11. Beach. 12. Whey.

94. 1. e. 2. f. 3. d. 4. c. 5. b. 6. a. 7. l. 8. j. 9. h. 10. i. 11. g. 12. k.

95. Cardiff. Cork. Dublin. Newport.

96. 1. The Beatles. 2. David Bowie. 3. Cliff Richard. 4. Scaffold. 5. Siren. 6. Plastic Penny. 7. Tom Jones. 8. Julie Andrews. 9. The Cream. 10. Elton John. 11. The Sweet. 12. Shirley Bassey.

97. 1. e. 2. k. 3. l. 4. f. 5. h. 6. i. 7. j. 8. a. 9. d. 10. c. 11. b. 12. g.

98. 1. Stomach. 2. Bicarbonate of soda. 3. A cut of beef. 4. Feet. 5. Grilled cheese on toast. 6. Stew. 7. Pickled in brine. 8. Starch. 9. Liver. 10. Herb. 11. Stewed. 12. Offal.

99. 1. Oak. 2. Ash. 3. Hawthorn. 4. Holly. 5. Beech. 6. Ivy.

100. 1. A small building in a garden. 2. A monolith. 3. Brown and white. 4. Spectacular, but sham buildings with no purpose. 5. a. 6. They were once private parks for deer-hunting. 7. A sunken wall or fence around a garden. 8. b. 9. A medieval tilting-post. 10. b. 11. A white horse. 12. Yes. It is a brick wall built in a wavy line.

The Armada Quiz and Puzzle Books

by Doris Dickens and Mary Danby

Boost your brain power and have hours of puzzling fun solving the hundreds of different quizzes in this popular Armada series.

Pick your favourite puzzle – names, pictures, anagrams, codes, magic squares, pets, mysteries, sport, history, spelling, doodles, and many, many more. Sharpen your wits and get puzzling!

Have you discovered Armada's latest quiz books? Facts and fun for everyone in some exciting titles:

Armada Horse & Pony Quiz Books
by Charlotte Popescu

Armada Football Quiz Books
The Armada Cricket Quiz Book
by Gordon Jeffery

The Armada Animal Quiz Book
by Deborah Holder

Car Quiz
by Hal Danby

The Armada Pop Quiz Book
by Maurice Kinn

The Armada Sky High Quiz Book
by Jack Stanger

The Great British Quiz Book
by Jonathan Clements

Armada

Armada Books of Fun
compiled by Mary Danby

Butler: The invisible man's outside
Lord Prune: Tell him I can't see him

I sat next to the duchess at tea;
It was just as I feared it would be:
   Her rumblings abdominal
   Were simply phenomenal,
And everyone thought it was me!

Two hilarious helpings of ridiculous riddles, riotous
rhymes, crazy cartoons and preposterous puns, let alone
loony limericks and jokes by the score!

And you'll find all your favourite cartoon characters in:
The Armada Book of Cartoons
and
The Second Armada Book of Cartoons

Laughs Unlimited!

Armada

Armada Crossword Books

compiled by Robert Newton

Are you a clued-up quizzler? Can you solve cunning clues quick as a flash? Here are ten terrific collections of 100 crosswords specially compiled for Armada. Pick up a pencil and fill in the answers!

And there's the extra game of clues and anagrams — **Starwords**—to add to the fun!

Armada

Armada Science Fiction

Step into the strange world of Tomorrow with Armada's exciting science fiction series.

ARMADA SCI-FI 1
ARMADA SCI-FI 2

Edited by Richard Davis

Two spinechilling collections of thrilling tales of fantasy and adventure, specially written for Armada readers.

Read about . . . The monstrous Aliens at the bottom of the garden . . . A jungle planet inhabited by huge jellies . . . A robot with a human heart . . . The terrible, terrifying Trodes . . . A mad scientist and his captive space creatures . . . The deadly rainbow stones of Lapida . . . The last tyrannosaur on earth . . . and many more.
Stories to thrill you, stories to amuse you—and stories to give you those sneaking shivers of doubt . . .

Begin your sci-fi library soon!

Armada

CAPTAIN ARMADA

has a whole shipload of exciting books for you

Armadas are chosen by children all over the world. They're designed to fit your pocket, and your pocket money too. They're colourful, gay, and there are hundreds of titles to choose from. Armada has something for everyone:

Mystery and adventure series to collect, with favourite characters and authors – like Alfred Hitchcock and The Three Investigators. The Hardy Boys. Young detective Nancy Drew. The intrepid Lone Piners. Biggles. The rascally William – and others.

Hair-raising spinechillers – ghost, monster and science fiction stories. Super craft books. Fascinating quiz and puzzle books. Lots of hilarious fun books. Many famous children's stories. Thrilling pony adventures. Popular school stories – and many more exciting titles which will all look wonderful on your bookshelf.

You can build up your own Armada collection – and new Armadas are published every month, so look out for the latest additions to the Captain's cargo.

If you'd like a complete, up-to-date list of Armada books, send a stamped, self-addressed envelope to:

Armada Books,
14 St James's Place,
London SW1A 1PF